MOUNTAIN

Smiles and

T
E
A
R
S

MOUNTAIN

SMILES and TEARS

CAROL STRAZER

Strazer Press

Red Feather Lake, Colorado

Strazer Press
Red Feather Lakes, Colorado

ISBN: 13:9780692892886

ISBN: 10:0692892885

PRINTED IN THE UNITED STATES OF AMERICA

For the love of God and my supportive husband, Bob, and our family of Michelle, Marcy, Mary Jean, Mark, Brian, Anthony, Austin, Duncan, Evan, Georgia Rose, Jack, Jonah, and Jacob.

Contents

MOUNTAIN

SMILES and TEARS

A Lifesaving Link

What if Bob or I get seriously ill? The question taunted us as we moved into our small log cabin, set on a granite ledge at 8,650 feet above sea level, in the Northern Colorado Rockies. We'd be living over 50 miles from the nearest city and more than an hour from the nearest hospital. Why was a 60-plus couple retiring in a remote area, even if the fishing was good? Part of the answer came when I traveled along our community's dirt roads to nearby Red Feather Lakes Community Library and discovered the helpful staff, free classes, and high-speed Internet access.

Glancing in the mirror one morning in 2007, I was surprised to discover a large bulge at the base of my neck. I pushed on it, and it was hard. *Maybe, therefore, I've been having difficulty swallowing,* I said to myself. After appointments with my local physician and a surgeon, I learned I had an enlarged, rapidly growing thyroid gland.

They recommended surgery to remove my thyroid and possibly my parathyroid as well.

What if I had cancer? I worried. What if the surgery injured my vocal cords? I'd had a friend who could only whisper after a similar surgery. Not long before, I had participated in a free medical information class taught at the library by an expert for the National Library of Medicine, who had traveled over two hours to get to us from the campus of the University of Colorado at Denver. The class had been especially helpful because we learned which Internet medical sites we could trust. I decided to use some of those sites to learn more about my condition and determine if I needed the surgery.

When I entered the library after my diagnosis, Sarah, the head librarian, immediately welcomed me. No matter how busy the staff and volunteers are, they're always there with a supportive presence and expert advice. I visited MedlinePlus (*medlineplus.gov*), a free consumer health information site, where I learned that removal of the parathyroid is not always necessary, and in most cases an enlarged thyroid is not cancerous—and even if it is, it's usually treatable.

The research reassured me, making me less fearful about what lay ahead. I decided that surgery was the best choice, and after the three-and-a-half-hour procedure, my surgeon explained that part of my small, butterfly-shaped thyroid gland had grown to the size of a grapefruit! One lobe had even grown into my lung, and other parts were pressing on my carotid artery and esophagus. Without the removal of the growths, I could have died.

Fortunately, my parathyroid gland was still intact, my vocal cords were fine, and the growths were not cancerous. With deep gratitude, I thanked God for excellent doctors, a supportive family and friends, and our little mountain library for all the help they gave me.

<0><0><0>

In partnership with *Woman's Day* magazine, the American Library Association asked readers to write about how their library had helped improve their health. At the time, the small library was having financial difficulties. When another library volunteer suggested the contest, it seemed like a way, besides volunteering, to help the Red Feather Lakes Community Library. Along with three other winners, "A Lifesaving Link" was printed in an article titled "The Library Made Me Healthier." It was in the March 3, 2009, issue of *Woman's Day* magazine.

Snow Falling Like Commas

Snow falling like commas,

On a blank page,

Dividing rocks and trees from poles,

Deleting nature's errors,

To begin a new document

Filled with hushed excitement.

Footprints, deeply embedded like words,

Create fresh paths from old tales.

A search for food, a phrase,

Then, pursuit and capture.

Coyotes howling success

Like writers

Hawking bestsellers.

You may wonder why I chose snow for my poem's subject. This spring, we've had many snowstorms, and our community's lake is still frozen. Even though it's mid-May, it snows, and my neighbors grumble as they shovel the slushy snow. The white aspen trees stand leafless. Near the mail shed, a shaggy moose chews on snow-encrusted willows, and two tiny hummingbirds shiver on my feeder. In the Northern Colorado Rockies at nearly 8,700 feet, winter is long—spring is short. Still, I love the snow, our small log cabin, and my family even more.

<0><0><0>

"Snow Falling Like Commas" earned a third-place prize and appeared in Eber and Wein's *Sunflowers and Seashells: Nature's Miles* (2010).

MIRACLE ON MICHIGAN AVENUE

Paralyzed, I am too terrified to move. As he screams horrible obscenities, he rockets around the room. Hopeful, my eyes seek the telephone, but he grabs it and rips the cord from the wall. My poor baby shrieks in terror—scared by the noise. I must protect her. In his fury, he kicks the desk chair, hurtling it against the wall. What if our assailant kicks my seven-month-old baby? I can't escape. Poor Mary fastened securely in her stroller, is between him and me. How can I get both of us out of here? Like cornered rats, my thoughts keep climbing on top of each other.

I should scream. But no one would hear me in this high-rise Chicago hotel. The windows are sealed. Since it is mid-afternoon, the housekeeper, business people, and other guests have left the floor. I scold myself for being so naïve as to answer and unlock the door—thinking my relatives were arriving early. Instead, this drug-crazed mugger shoved his way into our room. Who can protect us? I feel helpless.

Earlier, I'd visited my mother, a patient at Northwestern Memorial Hospital, a few blocks from our Michigan Avenue hotel. Pushing my baby in her stroller back to the hotel, I struggled to steer it against Lake Michigan's strong, wintery winds. Focusing on the weaving stroller, I didn't notice someone was following us.

When we arrived in our room, he appeared from nowhere, smelling of a sweaty, desperate rage. Now, I wonder if we'll die.

I pray, "Dear Lord, you gave me this gorgeous baby when the doctor thought I would miscarry. Please protect her now. Tell me what to do." Almost immediately, I feel less frightened.

What I hear is a strong, reassuring voice saying, "Talk—tell him why you're here." Although the answer seems strange, I begin talking in a high voice.

Ignoring my words, my assailant grabs at me, ripping my blouse, as he yells above my baby's cries. All I can see is his pock-marked face leering at me while his foul breath makes me want to vomit. Still, I'm grateful he is concentrating on me and not my poor child. If he doesn't hurt her, I don't care what happens to me.

Again, I hear the voice: "I am here to protect you. You do matter. Keep talking."

I talk, but my attacker doesn't seem to hear anything I say, as he keeps bellowing. I want to grab my baby and run. I want to escape to our Oregon home where my strong husband and wonderful teenage daughters wait for us, but we can't leave. He has us trapped.

"Please, please listen. We're here because my mother is in the hospital. She's very sick. She needs an operation, but they don't know if they can operate. Her heart is bad." I keep repeating the same words. My head is pounding; I gasp for breath as the words gush out. Words I can't hear because of his wild ranting. I keep praying for help. Even though I'm terrified, I feel a calm stillness separating me from his craziness.

He stops yelling. His thin, dark body ceases gyrating in its drug-induced state. Late-afternoon sunlight, filtered by heavy hotel curtains, catches in his single earring. Then, for a brief instant, his yellow bloodshot eyes stop darting and see mine. The tiny contact offers hope.

"Please," I beg. "Don't hurt my baby. She is scared." I keep pleading with him, trying to calm his rage.

Finally, whirling away from me, he angrily demands money. The coherence of his words, his first intelligible sounds, offers hope.

"Sure, anything." I grab my billfold on the dresser and give him all I have—forty dollars.

Before he leaves, he says, "If you open the door, I'll kill you." Then, he slams the door. Quickly, I lock it and open the door to my father's adjacent room. Even though my father is still at the hospital, I can use his phone, calling the front desk and asking them to notify the police. While I wait, hugging and soothing my baby, I thank God for His strength and guidance. Without His wise advice, something awful could have happened.

The following day, I identify my attacker by his unusual earring at a Chicago police station lineup. The detective says my assailant has been stalking and raping out-of-town visitors (believing they would soon leave the city and be unavailable to identify him).

The police quickly caught him because they had been staking out my hotel. When the concerned detective asks how I escaped rape, I tell him I just prayed and was told to talk to my attacker. Further, I explain I was afraid to fight for fear my baby would be hurt. He tells me I did the right thing by making a connection with the perpetrator — helping him see us as human beings and not as objects.

Since I don't want my assailant to hurt other women, I testify at a judge's preliminary hearing. When I call my worried husband in Oregon, his reassuring support comforts me.

Fortunately, I don't have to return to Chicago for my attacker's trial. Other witnesses provide convincing evidence, and he is convicted.

When I return home to Oregon and my Christian Family Class, I tell Sister about our miracle. "God calmed my fears, instilled courage, and helped me concentrate on what to do. The same day, police just happened to be staking out our hotel and were able to capture my would-be rapist." Sister nods wisely, as she hugs my precious baby, whose beautiful, almond eyes smile at us. Then, Sister whispers, almost like a benediction, "God will always protect us if we just ask Him."

<0><0><0>

Published in 2009, *Chicken Soup for the Soul: Tough Times, Tough People, 101 Stories about Overcoming the Economic Crisis and Other Challenges* by Jack Canfield, Mark Victor-Hansen & Amy Newmark.

This incident occurred while the author and her family lived, for twenty-nine years, in Lake Oswego, Oregon.

ODE TO A PLAIN MAN

I wanted a plain man—

An honest man who spoke truth,

A man who wouldn't wander

Seeking other women's lies,

A man who believed in hope and

Encouraged those with needs.

I wanted a good man—

A generous man who gave freely,

A man who didn't grasp fortunes

Seeking other men's approval,

A man who consulted his heart and

Helped those with needs.

I wanted a strong man—

A loving man who easily protected,

A man who wouldn't deny his family,

Seeking fortunes from corporations,

A man who cared for his children and

Provided for their needs.

I sometimes wonder—

What if I'd wanted a fancy man,

A man who lavished me with flattery,

Seeking my favor and trust,

A man who flirted with many,

But loved none but his needs?

I would have had words untrue.

So, even though praises are few,

And love notes I have not,

Expensive gifts rarer still,

I married a plain man—

He fulfilled my soul's desire!

<0><0><0>

This poem, written in 2017, commemorates the author and her husband's 55th wedding anniversary.

A RELUCTANT HELPER

"You're joking?" I said to my husband, Bob. "We have ten cords of wood to split and stack and more trees to cut, and now you want to do the neighbor's trees?"

"We should help. After all, our neighbor is a widow."

"But her family is coming for a visit, why couldn't they do it?" I smiled and hoped he'd agree.

He shook his head. No use arguing when he got that determined look—like one of the moose that refused to move aside from our mountain trails. I could feel resentment rising inside me as the summer heat melted my makeup. It wasn't fair that we needed to worry about our land and someone else's, too. Also, it wasn't right, the dry summer and frequent lightning had made us fearful of the wildfires that raged across Colorado.

We'd been lucky; I scolded myself. We could have lost everything in the recent High Park Fire—until then, the second largest and most expensive fire in Colorado's history. If the wind had changed direction, the fire could have hit us. A mere eight miles downwind, the fire destroyed more than 87,000 acres and 259 houses.

Some of our friends had lost their homes. One poor soul found out she was under-insured. She could never rebuild. Others had to itemize and value even the smallest of their lost possessions. It would take them more than a year before they could move forward.

Even though we had donated to the firefighters' fund-raising event, increased our insurance, and cleared all our dead trees, we felt powerless to protect ourselves from another fire. Still, we treasured our little piece of heaven— a small cabin facing the snow-topped peaks, with the wind shushing through the pines and the clouds clustering overhead.

We'd helped our church's deacon and his family remove burned trees and shrubs. Their home had survived the wildfire that surged up the hill and surrounded their house, but almost everything around it had not. Although the lawn chairs, made from recycled plastic, had melted to a handful of ashes, the nearby statue of Mary looked as pristine as when they'd purchased it.

Now, it was time to protect our property. I had stared at the scorched foundations of the dwellings near our deacon's home. The fire's intense heat had destroyed them in minutes but left other houses untouched. The High Park Fire's lessons seemed burned into my brain. The residences that survived had a firebreak, a clearing around their homes.

Near our home, we had nine healthy trees to fell. For years, we had sprayed, nurtured, and loved those trees. Although I hated to see them cut, it was necessary.

"At this rate, we'll be chopping down trees all summer. I wonder just how many seventy-year-old couples log trees," I grumbled under my breath. Still, we got our work done, and five days later, we arrived at our neighbor's house, just as her out-of-state relatives showed up. When they saw we had matters in hand, they planned a trip to town, some 90 minutes away.

Great, while we're felling their dead trees, they'll have a nice lunch at an air-conditioned restaurant, I thought. I prayed as I waved good-bye to them, "Oh Lord, forgive me for my un-Christian spirit."

Soon, Bob pointed where he wanted an enormous ponderosa pine tree to fall. When he jerked the chainsaw's rope, it roared to life. He placed the saw blade along the tree's trunk. After two neat cuts, a V-shaped wedge lay on the ground. He circled to the opposite side of the tree. Soon, his saw blade chewed a straight line to the point of the wedge. The tree wavered, struggled to stay upright, groaned and fell to the ground—exactly where he'd intended. We stared at the trunk's blue stain. It revealed how the drought and pine beetles had choked the life out of this magnificent, century-old ponderosa.

While Bob cut off the branches, I dragged them out from around his feet and neatly stacked them in a nearby pile. Felling trees and removing their limbs is dangerous work. I often imagined what I would do if Bob cut himself. I'd use the large kerchief he wore around his neck and a stick to make a tourniquet. It was something I'd learned long ago in Girl Scouts, and I wasn't certain I remembered exactly how. I hoped I wouldn't have to test my memory.

As Bob worked, I inhaled the pine trees' sweet smell of sap and admired the view. *At least, this is better than housework.* By the time we felled the last tree my sweaty hair stuck to my head. Perspiration ran into my ears. *Oh Lord,* I prayed, *if only the wind would blow.* I'd barely thought it when a soft breeze tickled my nose.

"Thanks," Bob said as he killed the chainsaw's engine and removed his ear plugs. "With you clearing away the slash, it made my job safer."

"Well, I didn't want you to trip and hurt yourself."

"I thought you didn't want to do this."

"It's okay. You were right. We needed to do this. Besides, I love being out in the woods and helping you."

A biblical verse about the man who refused to work, but then came and helped anyway, reminded me of myself.

Later, after a hot shower, I weighed myself. Those pounds I never could quite lose had been sweated off. I'd received my reward—along with a grateful friend's hug and my husband's kiss.

Looking out the window at white, doughy clouds lazing across the blue sky, I whispered, "Thank you for keeping us safe and for reminding me that it feels good to do the right thing—even if I am a reluctant helper.

MOTHER'S QUILT

Lightning struck all around.

Then, it hit the ground,

To ignite the High Park Fire.

With warnings that were dire,

Down the mountain, we sped,

While flames quickly spread.

My new home, how could I know,

Which way would the fire blow?

Too many houses burned that day—

That was all fire-fighters could say.

I searched through ashes and silt

But couldn't find my mother's quilt.

Dear Mother in Heaven above,

Forgive me: I've lost your prized love.

Of all the losses, I've known

This fire has surely shown,

With God's help, I could survive,

And forever, I would thrive.

<0><0><0>

Eber & Wein published "Mother's Quilt" in their *Best Poets of 2013*, volume 6. The summer of 2012 wildfires bloomed like Colorado's daisies. West of Fort Collins, Colorado, the High Park Fire raged from the initial lightning strike on June 9, 2012, until contained on July 1, 2012. High in the Rocky Mountains, many homeowners evacuated.

A friend's tragic experience inspired this poem. After evacuating once, she believed it was safe to return. Unfortunately, the fire changed direction. This time, with only minutes to evacuate, she left many of her belongings, including her mother's quilt. The fire destroyed her recently purchased home, her quilt, and most of her possessions.

A TIME TO HELP

When paralyzed with fear, some find it is hard to hear the truth.

It is September 7, 2009, and the radio airwaves, like rain drops, sprinkle more bad news about the serious recession. Gone are the euphemisms, such as the stock market's pullback, downturn, correction, and so on. Rising unemployment, foreclosures, business failures, and so forth are the news of the day.

Today on NPR, the broadcaster said since the recession began, volunteering has shrunk by 70 percent, the decrease in volunteers attributed to the nation's numerous economic problems. There are other justifiable reasons why people are no longer taking the time to help. What concerns me, though, is how many seem to have given up and become fixated on their problems.

You see, I believe in us. I know we can do remarkable things if we work together. The truth is, when we reach a friendly hand across fear's turbulent waters, we help not only someone else but ourselves. Helping others is empowering. Americans are recognized world-wide for their generosity. When we, as a nation, need help, the time has arrived to change our focus to assisting others.

It's not just about us, but everyone. Recently, I sent an e-mail via a nonprofit organization called the Institute for Justice and Democracy in Haiti, to former President Clinton, now UN envoy to Haiti. I asked him to support the release of a desperately ill, illegally imprisoned political prisoner. The poor man has languished in a Haitian prison for five years, waiting in wretched conditions for justice and a trial.

Instead of sinking in a quicksand of worry about our current problems, I did a small something. As a result, I found the energy to tackle another personal and community concern—the pine beetle–infested trees. I wrote a letter to our neighboring property owners, now living in Hawaii, informing them of their dying pine trees. Then, my husband and I helped a friend remove fifty beetle-killed trees from her property to help protect her house from wildfires. Following our example, another neighbor assisted her friends with cutting down their infected trees.

Like everyone, I worry about the Americans struggling to find work and make house payments. The numbers stagger my imagination. I, too, am concerned about dwindling savings, increased taxes, and inflation. There are many problems I can't solve, but I believe there will always be a cause, a person I can help. Even the smallest effort can make a difference. Won't you join me?

I SHOULD

I guess I should

Make the bed,

Shake out the rugs,

Take out the trash.

All the things I did

Yesterday and the day before,

But not today.

Today is poetry day.

A day I behold

Nature's promise of

Pelicans dipping their beaks,

To catch fleeing fish,

While a white-crested eagle

Swoops above at the ready,

For an unsuspecting fish.

Four majestic geese

Proudly honk and

Paddle by, two by two.

Winds weave the waves.

Mountain peaks,

Streaked by snow,

Reach for clouds

Lazing by and by.

No, today's duty is

To study the beauty.

Chores can wait.

AN UNUSUAL ART SHOW

Each one drifted into the cavernous space called the nursing home's dining room. Heads down, eyes averted, they crept slowly by, hoping no one observed them. A few residents easily propelled their wheelchairs to nearby round tables. Some, leaning over their walkers, struggled to move the heavy chairs, and then collapsed on them. A few murmured greetings. Some seemed in a daze, at this, my aunt's memorial service.

A soprano's singing, accompanied by a guitar's thrumming, softened the somber mood. The lilies' strong scents mingled with the aroma of food. On a linen-draped table lay an enormous basket of rolls near a colorful tray of cold cuts and cheeses. Bowls of nuts and mints were to the side of a tray piled with cookies. Some residents cast longing glances at the bounteous display, anxious for the ceremony to end.

In the front of the room stood my aunt's thirty-six paintings tacked to three large display boards. The paintings included flower arrangements interspersed with a few landscapes and even likenesses of buildings. Her subjects were reminiscent of her most admired artist Georgia O'Keefe but on a much smaller scale. Not one to spend money on enormous canvases, my aunt was both frugal and legally blind.

Some residents walked slowly by, admiring for the first time my elderly aunt's art. When they reached the pedestal with her eight-by-ten framed photo and her urn, they glanced quickly away as if they didn't want a reminder they, too, were approaching their life's ending.

Surely, in their long lives, they had attended many funeral services. Maybe, like my aunt, they had declined to participate in such sad occasions. Did her refusal to dwell on death or even plan a service, I wondered, contribute to her long life of ninety-eight years? Still, I hoped she would appreciate my efforts to provide a meaningful ceremony. The memorial was intended not only to celebrate her life but to heal those left behind. My aunt had few friends and family left, but she had many caregivers, helpers, and admirers.

Those of us who knew her well respected her many accomplishments, achieved before women's rights made it easier for women to access higher education. After her retirement as a university professor of education, Aunt Lois began painting, fulfilling a long-held dream from undergraduate days when she had minored in art. At the local senior center, she found a mentor who encouraged her painting.

During our frequent visits, she would begin the conversation with polite inquiries about our health and the family. Then she'd pause. The prelude was over. Now would come the main event.

With a smile and wave of her large hand, she'd say, "Would you like to see my latest painting?"

"Oh yes, definitely," we would reply.

Soon, she'd pull one canvas after another from her closet.

"See the magenta in this painting. I mixed it myself. I'm very good at colors. Most artists know so little about combining colors. Isn't that color just gorgeous? See how I accented the petals."

Only for a privileged few would she show her work. Although she would sometimes give away some of her art, she never displayed any on her walls. Few even knew she was an artist. For my aunt, I do not think anything fascinated her more than her paintings, except her manuscript for middle-school readers, which she wrote, researched, and edited, but never published. Her creative works gave her life purpose and meaning.

For those of us who loved her, I sometimes felt even she recognized how difficult she could be, especially during her last months, when bouts of dementia tested her tenacity and challenged her caregivers.

Abruptly, the minister interrupted my painful thoughts. He asked what words about my aunt I would like him to include. Well-accustomed to these events, he studied the obituary I'd written, memorizing details about someone he had never met. We chatted for a few minutes as he took notes. Although my aunt had never wanted a service, I wanted an official good-bye for the grand, but feisty, lady we loved.

For more than thirty years, we cared for her. We— my husband and I, the home's caregivers, residents, her banker, and her lawyer—deserved a ceremony to commemorate our admiring, and sometimes demanding, relationship with my aunt. We overlooked her shortcomings as we focused on her accomplishments and our love for her. I hoped my friends and relatives would do as much for me when I reached my life's end.

The minister rose and nodded to the singer whose voice softened to stillness. The harsh sound of the microphone called us to attention. The service began.

REMEMBER ME

They think I can't see,

And I can't hear.

But I see them look away.

I hear them say,

"She doesn't remember,"

And I disappear.

I feel their tension,

When they can't guess

The words I've lost.

And I feel stupid,

When I can't find

The bread I hid or

Write my name.

To hide my shame,

I say, "I love you."

At times, I get angry.

It's all I can do.

Sometimes I know

More than they do.

I see their looks of pity,

I don't want them.

I want their patience.

I want them to understand.

I want them to remember.

Once, I was a professor.

<0><0><0>

Based on the author's experiences caring for beloved family members suffering from dementia or memory loss and for others with similar problems and their caregivers, the author wrote this poem. Published in Eber & Wein's *Best Poets of 2011.*

BEAR AWARE TEAM

Spring in the mountains means the start of the bear season and the need for precautions to avoid enticing bears to human habitats.

In 2005, the Crystal Lakes Community at Red Feather Lakes recorded 122 bear incidents (42 in home entries). From 2000 to 2004, the bears had averaged more than 100 break-ins yearly. After numerous interventions, the Division of Wildlife concluded it needed a more effective preventive program.

At six feet, eight inches, husky DOW officer Jim Jackson looked ready to tackle anything, including offending bears.

"The bears can peel trailer doors like the lids of tin cans," he said. "They think trailers and homes are like McDonald's—fast food."

Bear damage often adds up to several thousand dollars.

"Too many of our neighbors are feeding the bears," Jackson said. "Feeding is leaving pet food and garbage, uncleaned barbecue grills and bird feeders out overnight."

The officer's talk mobilized the community, resulting in the Crystal Lakes Bear Aware Team. Linda Masterson, the author of *Living with Bears*, lent her expertise. Capably led by Jane and Jim Tiffin and Curt Livingston, with the support of the Crystal Lakes Road and Recreation Association, the team and DOW began an aggressive educational and surveillance program.

Early on, a bear, mistakenly identified as a rogue bear and captured live, was destroyed in compliance with DOW's policies. Since bears usually return or are killed by another bear whose territory it has invaded, experts do not recommend trapping and relocation. This bear's death, however, did not reduce the number of incidents.

Instead, this bear's execution energized the community as threats of fines had not. Few wanted to destroy a bear. Since the bears considered humans a friendly food source, the bears needed retraining or aversive conditioning. Recommended bear deterrents included unwelcome mats (plywood boards with screws or nails inserted up one-half inch and no more than two inches apart), air horns, portable electric fencing, and a pepper spray for bears (Counter Assault).

The number of bear incidents declined in 2006 to thirteen (twelve in homes). In 2007, there were no reports of bear problems.

It appeared the bear campaign was succeeding, until 2008. Then, a juvenile bear rudely awakened one Crystal Lakes camper family at four a.m. when the bear opened their unlocked car door and ravaged their food box. In Red Feather Lakes, a bear trapped inside a car caused $7,000 worth of damage. The bear had learned how to use outside car handles to get in but not inside handles to get out.

Despite nine bear incidents in 2008, CLBAT leaders and volunteers persevered. Noted for their expertise, they were invited to speak at and train other communities.

With 2009's mild winter and early spring, the bears have emerged a month early. In March, observers spotted two bears near Tesuque Trail and a bear on a house deck opposite Glacier View Gate One.

Residents in bear country are reminded to remove their bird feeders and garbage, store pet food, clean grills, and lock car doors.

For information on dealing with bears, contact the Fort Collins DOW office at 970-472-4300.

<0><0><0>

A version of the author's story ran in the May 2009 *North Forty News*. The monthly newspaper, founded in 1993, serves communities in northern Larimer County, Colorado, including Wellington, Timnath, and Fort Collins. The author's husband participated on the Crystal Lakes' Bear Aware Team.

One summer evening, the author and her husband discovered on their deck—a brown bear slurping nectar from their hummingbird feeders. After her husband chased the bear, not advised by this writer, he reluctantly left.

HIGH PARK FIRE

Lightning struck on June nine—

Smoldered for days, without a sign.

Now, wind-whipped, it devours

A hundred acres by an hour.

Flames leap into the sky.

Soon, someone will die.

Evacuate! Evacuate! In a flash,

Fifty-nine homes turn to ash.

Like hummingbirds, helicopters dip

Dangling buckets in ponds to slip

Back to the fires raging below,

And hope for clouds to rain, snow.

High Park Fire gains a national name,

Then, Waldo Canyon Fire steals its fame.

<0><0><0>

Colorado's fire, the High Park Fire, in 2012, was the national news' lead story. Soon, the terrible Waldo Canyon Fire claimed everyone's attention. Too many wildfires ate their way across the West. Fortunately, the High Park Fire spared the author's home and community.

<0><0><0>

Published in *International Who's Who in Poetry 2012.*

BECOMING CATHOLIC

I have avoided writing about this time of my life because it was too painful. At the time, the aching hollow feelings often threatened to surface, screaming so loudly I wondered if other people could hear them. Sometimes envied as a popular university student, instead of being happy, I was miserable. In fact, I was so depressed that death seemed attractive. No matter how much I accomplished, nothing seemed to fill my empty void or erase my self-hate. Friends, sorority sisters, family, even the school psychologist all tried their best, but to no avail.

Finally, I decided only God could help. I longed for a strong healing faith. I had visited churches of various religions with girlfriends and relatives. Praying for an answer, I suddenly remembered my aunt, whom I had attended mass with years ago. She was the first Catholic to join our extended family, and I marveled at her faith. Born with a crippled hip, she never complained. After she had married my uncle, she suffered numerous miscarriages before my cousin was born. Despite their many losses, my aunt's faith never wavered. Remembering her now, I recalled how I used to look forward to my visits to their Wisconsin dairy farm, eager to go to mass with her. Each Sunday morning, as my aunt and I knelt in prayer beneath the church's soaring arches, peace I had not known seemed to envelop me.

Observing my Catholic friends, including my roommate, I realized how much I admired them. They had something I did not. Their faith had made better people of them—they were confident, and they cared for others. I especially appreciated their attentive support as I struggled.

When I started dating my future husband, Bob, we had long discussions about religion and faith. One sunny fall afternoon as we sat alone in my sorority's living room, Bob said, "I hope you don't mind? Last night, I kept thinking about you, so I wrote this little poem." He smiled his warm smile. "Remember, I'm studying engineering, not English like you."

Looking at the small hand-written note, I read the refrain, "Carol is like a leaf floating down a stream . . ."

I sat very still, stunned.

"You're not mad or anything?"

"Oh Bob, you understand. And now I understand. I've been trying to please everyone, parents, teachers, and friends. I feel overwhelmed, guilty and frustrated. It's too much. I don't know which way to go!"

"I understand," Bob said as he wrapped his arms around me.

During the next few weeks, I prayed and frequently thought about our talk. I listened and what I heard was, "The Catholic Church will help you find what is important, what God wants." For the first time, I felt embraced by safe boundaries and forgiveness. The Catholic Church was a theology on which I could depend to pardon my guilt. Harming oneself was a sin. I could close the door on those thoughts.

I began to feel more alive, almost as if I suffered from frostbite and now I was tingling with a new faith. I could feel a presence, a love touching me, not for what I did, but who I was. After taking lessons in the Catholic faith, a year later, in front of family and friends, I was baptized Catholic. For the first time, I felt safe and secure, trusting in my new faith.

It has been more than forty years since I joined the Catholic Church. With counseling, prayer, study, and a loving family, I have found a miraculous life. It hasn't always been easy being Catholic. And it hasn't always been easy being me. I am not perfect. I have made mistakes and had my doubts, but the Catholic Church has always been there to welcome me home.

Now, as I celebrate mass with Bob, my patient husband of forty-five years, I pray for our three beautiful daughters, their husbands, and our three grandsons. During the summer months, Bob and I help at our small mountain Catholic mission church, Our Lady of the Lakes.

We usher, lector, distribute communion, publicize services, and even clean the church. We hope others experience the healing faith, hope, and sense of direction that I found as a Catholic.

<0><0><0>

This story was written and submitted to *Chicken Soup for the Soul: Living Catholic Faith.* The submission guidelines recommended that the story should be a first-person, true account of how the Catholic religion had instilled hope, inspired faith, and encouraged love. As a long-ago convert to Catholicism, the writer thought her story might have a different slant than other submissions. "Becoming Catholic" was published in 2008 in *Chicken Soup for the Soul: Living Catholic Faith, 101 Stories to Offer Hope, Deepen Faith, and Spread Love,* by Jack Canfield, Mark Victor Hansen & LeAnn Thieman.

A SUNNY SNOW DAY

Trees grasping snowballs

In their piney boughs.

Hot sun bears down,

Until a ball is released,

To fall like a collapsed cake,

On creamy snow below.

Snow shyly shrinks aside

To reveal a log, a rock.

Melting snow once

Puffy with man's dreams.

Now, soggy and soiled

With heated reality.

Still, I'll gather

Snow drops,

And savor a sunny snow day.

BEST FRIENDS ARE FOREVER

One bright, Midwestern spring day, I walked home alone from shopping downtown. Passing by my best friend Monica's apartment, I noticed her mother's '52 Chevy parked by the curb, windows suspiciously fogged up, and two recognizable heads are bobbing inside. Though embarrassed, I stared at the steamy windows. Like a huge billboard, I imagined a sign announcing *Carol's Ex-Boyfriend Is Dating Her Best Friend*.

Hoping they didn't see me, I raced home, ran upstairs to my room, and threw myself on the bed. "How could my friend and ex-boyfriend be making out?" I asked my angel fish swimming gracefully back and forth in their tropical aquarium. I felt as they might feel if they had swallowed a baited hook and wanted to throw up. How could I have been so stupid not to see this coming?

When we first met as fourth-graders, I felt sorry for Monica. She'd suffered much tragedy. Her twin brother had died when she was very young. On her nightstand was a photo of her deceased father. Unlike his rather plain and light-haired daughter, Monica's father had been darkly handsome; his picture reminded me of a movie star.

Monica had several eye operations to correct her crossed eyes and wore thick glasses. Since I, too, had eye problems and wore ugly glasses, I could identify with her.

Soon, Monica and I found many other similarities. We were both new in town and lonely. Monica's mother had taught at a country school, and they had lived on a farm. When the local elementary school hired her mother to teach, they moved to an apartment in town. Like Monica's, my family had recently relocated, moving from Wisconsin to Illinois. My father had a new job. Our ancient Victorian house, which my mother was desperately trying to rescue from its overgrown jungle, was conveniently located across the street from Monica's apartment building.

We discovered many common interests: reading, playing games, and imagining stories. Although a year younger than me, Monica had skipped a grade and was in my class. Sometimes, curly-headed Monica would help me with my math problems. Since Monica's teacher-mother often worked late, we frequently played and studied alone, undisturbed in their cozy apartment while munching on stale Halloween candy her mother left out for us. Having smart Monica as a best friend made me feel special. I liked and admired her. In fact, she was my only friend, and since my parents and much younger twin sisters had busy social lives, Monica became family.

Now, tears washed down my face. I'd trusted Monica and recalled our recent conversation as we walked to school.

"Monica, can you believe Jerold wanted to kiss me? And more than that, he wanted me to come over to his house when his parents weren't there to play some weird kissing and bondage games. I refused. I couldn't believe he'd suggested such a thing. His mother was my favorite Sunday school teacher. I would never be able to look her in the eye. I think I should break up with Jerold. What do you think?"

Monica adjusted her glasses and looked down at the sidewalk. When she raised her head, her magnified lenses made her eyes look huge as she stared at me. "You're right," she said. "You shouldn't have to put up with his weird stuff. Dump him."

Monica never told me she wanted my boyfriend. Feeling betrayed, I scolded myself for being so trusting. Once I had looked forward to eighth grade, but now, everything was a disaster. I felt so hurt. I couldn't imagine ever again getting close to a friend. I avoided Monica, and she didn't call me. Our friendship ended.

During the next few years, I focused most of my displeasure on myself—believing I was unworthy of friends. What began as an ex-friend's punishment became my jail sentence. Eventually, Monica and I graduated from high school and went our separate ways.

Finally, years later, I decided to call Monica. I'd returned to my hometown for another visit. Monica had completed business school, found a job, and married someone else. They had five children. I, too, had married, was teaching and had moved to another state.

It felt like old times as we chatted, with neither of us mentioning the long-forgotten Jerold. I had missed my friend and regretted it had taken me so long to forgive her and reconnect. How foolish I had been. Boyfriends come and go, but a best friend is forever.

A few years later, I received a letter from my mother. Still living in my hometown, she kept me informed about the local news. As I opened the envelope, a newspaper clipping fell out. I studied it, not wanting to believe what I read. But it was true. My best friend had died, killed in a terrible two-car accident. Frantically, I called my mother hoping it was a mistake, but it wasn't, and she told me the gruesome details. I was devastated.

Recently, while shopping, my mother said she met Monica's oldest daughter, Cynthia, who was with her grandmother. When Mother expressed her condolences at their loss, a teenaged Cynthia said, "Mother always said, 'Carol was my best friend.'" When my mother repeated

Cynthia's words, my heart hurt as I regretted my long overdue act of forgiveness and mourned the years we'd lost. Never did I regret the loss of my relationship with Jerold. I had been too immature for romance while, obviously, Monica was not. Still, grieving, I could see I had been too proud to say anything.

At least, I consoled myself we'd forgiven each other and reconnected. As I looked up at the white clouds sailing swiftly by, I said, "I will never forget you, Monica. You taught me an important lesson—forgiveness and friendship are more important than pride and safety."

Best friends are forever.

GOD'S THOUGHTS

Share Your thoughts,

You, I've sought.

My soul lingers, O Lord,

At your feet in solitude.

My thoughts fly around.

They send me aground.

But your thoughts, O Lord,

Fill me with gratitude.

With hope in You anew,

My life can renew.

I gave so little for you, O Lord,

You gave me a new view.

Your thoughts are glorious;

They sing like a chorus.

Teach me Your ways, O Lord,

To live the Beatitudes.

A DANGEROUS JOURNEY

The wind whipped my face as I clutched, with sweaty palms, a single cable stretched above the rocks. Any movement caused gravel to fall silently over the precipice to the valley far below. There, the cars had shrunk to the size of my grandson's toys. If I lost my grip, nothing would prevent me from falling. While recalling the stories of some hikers' fatal falls, jets from the nearby air force base screamed overhead, distracting me.

Afraid to move, I considered going back, but that was impossible. The narrow two-foot ledge didn't allow enough room to turn around. What if I couldn't hang on to the cable? What if the cable came loose? What if I slipped and fell? If only there were a safety harness, rope, and some protection. Powerless, I stared at the sharp rocks far below me.

When my husband Bob and I started up Arizona's Picacho Peak, I thought it would be like the other hikes we usually did, a long walk up and down a mountain. Even the stories we'd heard about some hikers falling to their deaths, I'd discounted as exaggerations. This hike had become something entirely different—a rock climb, without safety gear. Neither of us had trained in rock climbing. Too late to turn back, I regretted my decision to hike.

My husband, who'd safely navigated the trail's dangerous stretch, yelled back at me, "Don't look down! Don't look down!"

"Okay," I gasped, afraid that even talking would cause me to slip.

"You can do it. Just put one foot in front of the other. Don't let go. Slowly slide your hands along the cable. That's it. You can do it. You can make it," he coaxed.

Following his instructions, I'd made it. He'd saved my life.

Now, years later, I try to emulate his patient support and help him. Change is scary. He deserves my respect and love. Ever since his diagnosis of polycystic kidney disease, PKD, my fears for his health have been driving me: to check food labels for too much sodium, to make more homemade soups and salads, and even to hide the salt shaker. When he'd complain, he'd receive a lecture on the benefits of a healthy diet. Still, I didn't want to drive him away from me. In my mind, Bob's health had come first, but truly, our marriage was more important. We often talk about how we can be more loving. Fear has no place in a caring relationship. Trust and respect do.

Now, I encourage my husband more and remind him less. When he occasionally slips, I remember climbing those slippery rocks, step by step. He needs my patience and to take a break from his diet. Recently he saw his doctor, who was amazed at Bob's vastly improved blood tests and predicts Bob's kidneys will last for many years. The doctor's response convinced Bob that we are on the right path.

Our love for each other thrives as together we face what sometimes seems like life's dangerous journey. No longer climbing peaks, we walk gentler paths. Change may be scary, but if we keep our focus and don't look down, together, we'll make it.

<0><0><0>

In 2003, the author and her husband sold their Oregon home and began traveling. With their Chevy truck pulling a small travel trailer, they headed east to care for her husband's mother in Waukegan, Illinois. When she passed away, they drove to Arizona, camping at various RV parks. With their good friends from high school days, Joann and George, they explored Arizona and had many adventures—including climbing Picacho Peak.

IT'S HARD TO BELIEVE

There is no sound except

Pine trees breezily sighing,

Now they grow brown—

Those once emerald green.

It's hard to believe tiny bugs

Strangle these mighty pines.

Ponderosa, lodge pole, and limber, too,

Succumb, await chainsaw or fire.

Some say, "It's nature's way." Is it?

Heat and drought caused by what?

Three million are dying or dead,

Fuel for future forest fires.

Twenty years from now,

Forgotten, like the pine beetle,

I'll lie buried near my friends and

Make way for tomorrow's promise.

A MOTHER'S LOVE

I watched in horror as televised images displayed a violent Haitian demonstration preventing the U.S. troop ship from docking at Port-au-Prince. The international military trainers couldn't disembark. Their mission was to facilitate President Aristide's return to Haiti and to restore order and safety for the terrified Haitian citizens. October 1993 was just two years after a military junta had ousted Jean-Bertrand Aristide, the first democratically elected Haitian president in 200 years.

What will happen to our daughter Marcy, I wondered? Dear God, I prayed, please protect her. As a human rights observer, Marcy worked for the Organization of American States (OAS). They assigned her to the city of Hinche, in Haiti's Central Plateau. The paramilitary and often the military routinely subjected Haitian citizens who supported democracy to beatings, imprisonment and even death. Some Haitian citizens risked arrests and brutal reprisals just to tell their stories to the OAS. Marcy documented the human rights abuses, visited prisoners, and confronted notorious military chiefs, such as Captain Zed, about violations and abuses.

Inspired by the Haitians' courage, Marcy disregarded her safety to serve them, though she feared for *their* lives. I worried about my daughter who took such dangerous chances to help others, first as a Peace Corps volunteer in Zaire (renamed the Democratic Republic of the Congo) and now in Haiti. Even as a child Marcy had been sensitive to the needs of the forgotten. Before social services became involved, six-year-old Marcy often invited two neglected, little girls home for dinner.

Each day I anxiously followed radio and television news reports and wondered what I could do to protect her. When an early-morning broadcast mentioned a possible U.S. evacuation from Haiti of American citizens and said the White House was studying the public's response, I rejoiced. Finally, besides praying, I could do something. The kitchen clock read seven a.m. Pacific Time which would be ten a.m. Eastern Time. I could call and still be on time for my job as the hospital's community health educator.

While I waited for an answer, I prayed. "Oh Lord, please help my call go through and let it not be too late to vote."

"Hello, this is the White House. May I help you?" a melodious voice asked. I gasped. I couldn't believe it. A real person answered—not a machine. I thought I'd better talk fast because this person was probably very busy. "Hello," I spit out, "I just called to cast my vote to evacuate American citizens from Haiti, and my daughter is there."

The kind lady responded, in a voice that reminded me of mint juleps and magnolias. "My goodness, you all must be worried. I know I would be if my daughter was in the middle of that mess. Where do you live?"

"Oregon."

"What a coincidence. My new son-in-law is from Oregon. It must be beautiful there."

"It is. You'll have to . . ."

She interrupted me to say, "Oh, President Clinton just walked by discussing Haiti."

Astonishing! History was in the making. I felt as if I was in another world. Unhurried, the operator asked for Marcy's name, location, agency, and then my name and phone number.

"Don't worry," she reassured me. "I think the president will make a decision soon."

Repeatedly thanking her, I hung up and grabbed my car keys and briefcase. Why didn't I think to ask her name? Turning on the car's ignition, I prayed, "Lord thank you for sending me an angel. Please protect my daughter and all those helping the Haitians."

Several days later, the television newscaster announced the evacuation of American citizens from Haiti. Soon, I received a phone call.

"Mom, I'm okay. They sent a plane. A lady came down the ramp and asked if I was Marcelle Strazer. When I said 'yes,' she said, 'Call your mother.' I couldn't believe it. I was embarrassed. When the OAS informed us, we had to leave I had to destroy all our documents to ensure the military didn't get them. And we had to get the two Haitians who helped us with cooking and other chores into hiding."

Marcy talked nonstop. I could barely squeeze in my question. "Why?"

"The FRAPH (paramilitary) would kill them. It's bad over there. You can't imagine how those poor people are suffering. I'm in the Dominican Republic. I'll be here for a while, writing my reports. People are waiting for the phone. I'll call back later. Bye."

Before Marcy clicked off, I managed a quick "I love you." And then, replacing the receiver, I said, "Thank you, God." Relief, gratitude, and love enveloped me. Tears flowed as I shared the wonderful news with her worried father and two sisters.

When the family wanted to know more about where Marcy was in the Dominican Republic, we studied a map of the Caribbean island of Hispaniola. Haiti, among the West's poorest countries, was located on the island's western shores. The Dominican Republic, once owned by Spain, covered more than half the island. With a stable government, the Dominican Republic's economy was more prosperous and the country safer.

I may have embarrassed my adventurous daughter, but I didn't care. After all, it is a mother's right to protect her family with prayers, faith, and, when all else fails, even a call to the White House.

A WORD

A word, a single syllable,

A word said in a second.

Fragile as a dove,

Power of an eagle's wings,

A word all have heard.

Say it and hope begins.

Pray it, and He enters.

Believe and be healed

By love forgiving,

Just a word,

God.

MY NEW BEST FRIEND

My husband Bob and I took turns puffing on our last cigarette until all I held was a charred filter. In a nearby planter, I partially buried it with other cigarettes. They reminded me of miniature headstones. Gazing sadly at the tiny cemetery, I said farewell to my best "friend" of twenty-two years.

We, my cigarette and I, met the summer before my senior year in high school. Terribly shy, I was delighted when classmates invited me to a summer picnic at the city park. After lunch, the other girls lit up. "Wow," I thought, "this is grown-up stuff." I pictured sophisticated ladies holding cigarettes between polished nails while dashing gentlemen flicked silver lighters.

When a friend asked me if I would like a drag on her cigarette, I readily accepted. Soon, she corrected my crude attempts, saying, "Inhale and exhale, like this."

"This is easy," I told myself. "All I have to do to be accepted is smoke." By dusk, all I wanted was a cigarette.

In the decades that followed, I smoked at least 154,000 of those gleaming white tubes of tobacco. I could always depend on my "friend" to give me a boost, calm my fears, or blow away my anger.

My doctor disagreed. He said my friend gave me bronchitis, asthma, and poor circulation. When he said my buddy and I would have to part, tears filled my eyes and I choked out, "Really?" He just nodded.

Following his orders, I tried to quit and refused to buy any more cigarettes. If I didn't have them around to tempt me, I reasoned, I wouldn't smoke.

Still, when smoking friends visited and left my home, I grabbed the ashtrays, searching for viable butts to smoke. Flashbacks of Seattle's Skid Road's homeless retrieving discarded smokes from the dirty sidewalk flashed through my memory as I chided myself.

Gaining weight, eating instead of smoking, caused me to give in and buy cigarettes. Skewered on the adage "Quitting smoking is easy, I quit many times," I couldn't resist my cigarette "friend's" siren call.

Lunching with a former smoker, she reinforced my guilt and frustration when she inquired about my attempts to quit smoking.

"You know I quit," she said. "I don't even think about it. When I decide to do something, I do it. No problem, easy as pie."

I stared at her, secretly imagining throwing a pie at her.

At another lunch, this time with a friend who still smoked, I heard, "I know I should quit. But this isn't the time. You know the divorce and all."

I thought that getting a divorce would be a perfect excuse to keep smoking.

I tried every stop-smoking technique I knew. Once I quit for three weeks, but always found a good excuse to start again. Also, my husband was determined to stop. I thought if we both quit at the same time, it might be easier. When I heard a local church was sponsoring a smoking cessation program, we signed up.

Bob and I snuffed out our "last" cigarette and entered the church auditorium. After the program director's brief introduction, the room darkened, and scenes from an actual lung cancer operation flashed on the screen. The grim images erased all desire I had for cigarettes that night.

Terrifying facts may work for a while, but we learned it takes more than fear to erase an addiction. Successive nights of instruction bolstered our weak intentions. We learned more about tobacco's harmful effects and healthy alternatives to smoking. Fellow smokers supported our efforts.

When our leader suggested asking for God's assistance, I realized it was one technique I had not tried.

I begged God for His help. Without His intervention, I knew I would smoke again.

In the morning, when I craved a cigarette with my coffee, I prayed. When a friend offered me a cigarette, I prayed . . . And I refused. After dinner, when a cigarette would have tasted the best, I prayed—always the same prayer. "Lord, I'm helpless. Please help me. I can't quit." And I truly believed I couldn't.

Early one morning I woke, prepared coffee, and drank an entire cup before I realized . . . I hadn't craved a cigarette! Astonished, I held my empty cup and looked out the window. To the dawning sky I whispered, "You did it, Lord. You did it! Thank you!"

It had been three weeks, just when I usually started smoking again. My craving for cigarettes had died. Before, my nicotine addiction had screamed for relief. Now, there was silence. I could live without cigarettes.

Later, helping a group of anxious smokers, I told them how many times I'd failed to quit. I recounted my winning technique: I asked for God's help, and He answered my prayer.

Thirty years later, I live high in the Colorado mountains where I hike, kayak, and ski with my husband and grandchildren. I'm free—no longer a slave to cigarettes, thanks to "My New Best Friend."

<0><0><0>

This story was published in 2011 in *Chicken Soup for the Soul: Answered Prayers, 101 Stories of Hope, Miracles, Faith, Divine Intervention, and the Power of Prayer,* by Jack Canfield, Mark Victor Hansen, and Ann Thieman. "My Best Friend" was originally submitted under another title for *Chicken Soup for the Soul: Miracles.* When it wasn't accepted, the story was sent to *Chicken Soup for the Soul: Answered Prayers.* The back cover of *Chicken Soup for the Soul: Answered Prayers* notes how the author overcame her addiction to cigarettes with prayer.

FIERY LOVE

Jesus, I hear you calling,

You whisper my name.

Shattered and unwanted,

I thought I was all alone.

No one cared but you

Until you spoke and said,

I am here to give you rest.

Look not for others.

They have gone away.

Look for me to give you peace,

To give you hope, and love.

Only I know how to forgive

And save your soul to live.

If you love me, you will give

Your heart that burns for me.

Oh Lord, take my heart,

Fill it with your love.

So, I might be like you.

Shape me in your ways

To follow only you.

Teach me that I belong

In your home where I yearn to be.

My heart is on fire with your love.

NEVER TOO LATE TO WRITE

Over our commode hangs an oil painting of a tall, gray Grecian urn beside a small, round lavender vase. An ornate, silver letter opener lies next to them on top of an open envelope and a letter. Since the envelope is face down, I can't read the return address. Probably it isn't mine, but I wonder.

Lately, I've thought of moving my mother's painting to a more honored location, a place our guests could admire it. Instead, I've left it here in our master bathroom, because the painting's painful loneliness was too personal to share. Letters wished for—especially from her eldest daughter— but rarely received. Even though I admire her perfect artistry, the painting is a reminder of my mother's sad regrets.

After she had died, two paintings were all we found; we wished that there were more. My sister claimed one. When I took Mom's other painting home, I recalled what my mother had said years before: "If only I could have finished college. I loved to paint." Instead, her dad said he couldn't afford for her to complete her art degree. She'd have to give up her dream, return to the farm, and care for her asthmatic mother.

In my sixties and with grown children, I often wondered whether I would end up like her. If, after my funeral, my children might clean out my home and be surprised to find my unpublished writings. Mother's painting made me feel culpable. It seemed that she had given up her artistic gifts to raise my sisters and me, in much the same way I had relinquished my desire to write.

Still, I didn't understand: When we left for school, husbands, and careers, why didn't she pursue her art? Was it because of a loss of confidence, a fear of failure, or a husband's demands? I'll never know.

What I do know—the painting I claimed was the greatest bequest she could have given me. I'd dreamed of writing forever, but other responsibilities took precedence.

Crafting stories seemed like a forbidden indulgence, but her painting sent me a relentless message. It was time.

After I had retired, I volunteered to write, and later edit, our community newsletter. The staff were desperate; I was free. Besides editing, I found my niche in interviewing and writing about new residents. I attended a writing class and then a writers' conference. It wasn't easy. And family responsibilities, especially caring for my elderly aunt in faraway Oregon, weighed heavily. It was tough to find the time.

Even if I rose early and wrote, there were always interruptions. Still, my husband and friends encouraged me. I studied writing books and magazines and worked with a writing coach. I submitted a few stories and was surprised when one was accepted. I cried. Maybe I was—I could be—a writer. It still didn't seem possible. I had so much more to learn.

To surround myself with books and revel in other authors' successes, I volunteered at our small library. A friend suggested that I enter a writing contest sponsored by

Woman's Day and the National Library Association. I did. When I received a call from New York telling me I'd won, I was stunned. Naïvely, I assumed *Woman's Day* hadn't received many entries. "Oh no," the caller said. "We had sacks and sacks of stories, but we liked yours. It was well-written." Choked up, I could barely thank her. Next, I submitted a story to our local newspaper. When they printed it with a photo, I began to feel like a real writer. Almost.

To improve, I would have to overcome my fear of criticism. As a child, when my mother criticized me, I took it personally. At the time, I didn't understand she lacked the patience and awareness of how to teach me—her overly sensitive daughter—in the way, I needed to comprehend.

Still, I would need more support to overcome my fears. Since there wasn't a local writers group, I helped organize one. The group provided structure and skill building. Then, we invited experienced writers to give seminars to our group and rural community. Encouraged by other writers, one's trust and talent grow.

One group member, whose pastor husband had advanced Parkinson's disease, inspired us with her courageous poetry. Other participants, many of them caregivers, endured enormous challenges to their writing. Most persevered. For me, constructive criticism no longer felt like a devastating emotional attack. Even more important, like my mother, I found my Christian faith renewed my courage. "Pray and write" became my mantra.

After seven years, I finished researching, writing, and publishing a historical fiction book, *Barbed Wire and Daisies*. Based on a little-known story from World War II about a German mother and her four young children who fled the advancing Russian army, the family faced starvation, illness, mistreatment, and heart-rending conditions in Danish refugee camps.

Now, when I speak to various groups, often someone will say, "I've always wanted to write my story, but I'm too old," or "It's too late." I tell them that it's not true. In this digital age, there are many choices possible to self-publish a book. There are e-book formats or services such as Amazon's CreateSpace. I tell wannabe writers how to find writers' groups, classes, and conferences that can advance their learning. There are Christian writers' conferences. There are editors, coaches, designers, and other professionals to help them with publication. I recommend that they subscribe to writing magazines such as *Writer's Digest* or *The Writer* and explain how to search *Writer's Market* or *The Christian Writer's Market* to find places they can submit their work. And I tell them that if I can do it, anyone can.

Sadly, I think of those who may never write their great stories. A reader of my book told me his story. As a boy in Germany, he survived World War II but endured many hardships. Orphaned, he'd been adopted and came to America. Before she passed away, his wife wrote his story and placed it, along with photos and maps, in a loose-leaf notebook. I'm certain their only daughter is as happy to have his story as I am to have my mother's painting.

Dear Mom, thank you for reminding me it is never too late to write. Oh yes, and you will be relieved to hear your painting is no longer in our bathroom. It's now prominently displayed in our living room.

<0><0><0>

Published in *Christian Living in the Mature Years,* Spring 2016.

WRITING IS LIKE KAYAKING

Writing is like kayaking.

Courage is a needed oar

To shove one's fragile craft

Into icy waters of self-doubt.

Other brave kayakers,

Like writers encourage trust,

Reach beyond a safe shore,

Risk the unknown waters.

To overcome paralyzing fears,

To challenge critical feedback,

To maneuver class V rapids,

And return to wiser words.

Trust in the *greatest kayaker*

To lead beyond the *word*.

<0><0><0>

Published in *Best Poets of 2014*, vol. 2. In addition to writing, the author enjoys hiking and kayaking.

JUST ONE MORE HILL

If you were to meet Helain, you'd never suspect the arduous journey she has traveled. For many summers, her lithe figure easily ascended the steep trails as she set our hiking group's pace. We might gripe about sudden rain showers, over-grown trails, and high altitudes, but Helain never complained. Her smiling face, surrounded by silver-tinged blonde hair, always encouraged us. Big deal, you might say, she sounds like any good leader.

Helain's story is not that of a typical hiker. In early 2010, she received the diagnosis most women fear—breast cancer, something she hoped to avoid by adhering to a healthy diet, weight bearing exercise, purified water, and health supplements.

In fact, concerned about the risk of x-rays, for eight years Helain had avoided getting a mammography. After all, she had not found a lump or had any problems.

When she finally had a mammography and then a follow-up visit, the results were not encouraging. After a subsequent needle biopsy and further tests, she was told that her cancer was considered a ductal carcinoma in situ (DCIS), believed mild. Although stunned by the diagnosis, Helain felt reassured. Recently, she had read that the cancer was not considered life threatening.

Determined not to let her condition interfere with her lifestyle, she continued to do the things she loved, including participating in her usual Bible study and intercessory prayer meetings. The scripture passage she found most helpful was, "Call upon me in the day of trouble. I will deliver you, and you will glorify me" (Psalm 50:15) (*WEB*). Helain said, "That was my word from God to glorify God."

In answer to her prayer for the right surgeon — someone she could "bond with" — Helain found a doctor with a positive and friendly manner that comforted her.

On the day of her lumpectomy, she and her in-laws fasted while her pastor prayed for her. The surgeon operated on her breast. He also removed two lymph nodes and additional tissue. After her surgery, Helain was amazed that she felt no pain. She did not even require a pain pill.

Several days later, the pathologist's report indicated invasive carcinoma, grade 3, as well as a high-grade of ductal carcinoma. Her condition had not been completely evident in her tests. Instead of fear, Helain received the news with unusual gratitude. She said, "I was grateful for the information which had been hidden; the Lord had brought to light."

Her surgeon asked if she wanted a double mastectomy, but Helain declined, opting to remove only one breast. If cancer reappeared later in the second breast, it would be mild, as when first identified.

Once again, she sought encouragement from her prayer group and religious leaders. The day of her surgery, she read Joel Osteen's book. He described how during violent storms flexible palm trees bend and are not uprooted as easily as mighty oak trees. She would be like the resilient palm tree and "bounce back." Adversity would strengthen her. "The righteous shall flourish like the palm tree. He will grow like a cedar in Lebanon" (Psalm 92:12) (WEB). With the support of her faithful husband Kevin, her family, and friends, Helain had surgery.

Her mastectomy and reconstruction were successful. Later, when a positive pathology report recommended no further treatment, she rejoiced. It was an answer to her prayer.

If only her story ended there. Insted *the cancer had returned!*

In 2011, ultrasounds, biopsies, and further tests at her six-month check-up showed stage 4 cancer. It was inflammatory and spreading fast. It had traveled from her left breast to her right breast, across her chest, to the lymph nodes under both her arms and up her neck. The skin on her chest was blotchy from cancer. Her doctor said, "Since this is a very aggressive cancer, you may not want to do anything."

Helain responded, "I want to fight it."

Her oncologist said, "The drug I'm going to use on you may not work. If it doesn't, we'll try something else."

"Oh, it will work," Helain replied. "There are a lot of people praying for me."

"Keep that attitude," her doctor said.

When Helain shared the news of cancer's reoccurrence with some of us hikers, we gasped. Our eyes filled with tears. We tried not to stare at the raw, radiated flesh above her blouse's opening. We could see this was her greatest challenge. Helain continued hiking. Cancer would not stop her. Some of us promised prayers and were relieved when we learned that she belonged to a women's cancer support group.

The group of 12 to 15 women met at a local restaurant, shared prayers, their stories, and frequent laughter. In between their meetings, they took each other to appointments and provided needed help.

Helain continued to pray and seek support from her friends, ministers, family, and even her email contacts. This time, more tests revealed good news. Her cancer had not spread to her bones or her vital organs. She had a strong immune system. Her doctor told her she had "the heart of an eighteen-year-old." Since she had heard many patients suffered heart attacks during their treatments, this was good news.

When Helain went to her chemotherapy appointments, she found the doctors and nurses to be especially loving and caring. Instead of fearing the sessions, she welcomed them as she listened to inspirational tapes, read, and rested. After four months of chemotherapy, the PET scan showed complete and total remission of her cancer. Her doctor continued the treatments.

Despite everything, Helain continued to lead the weekly hikes. Some treks were even ten miles. She also kept her other commitments. For twenty-six years, she had led praise and worship services at the local county jail and the Cañon City prisons.

For two-and-a-half years, Helain endured a long series of radiation and chemotherapy treatments. Her upbeat attitude was evident as she repeated her doctor's words: "You're doing better than all of my other patients with inflammatory breast cancer."

Helain is grateful that she has had little pain or nausea and is only now experiencing some hair loss. She cautions others to remember that a good diet, exercise, and healthy living are not always insurance against cancer. As Helain puts it, "A carrot can't cure cancer."

She says, "You don't fool around with cancer. It's a demonic disease. Each time it returns, it arrives with a vengeance." She reminds women to keep their annual mammogram appointments.

In late July her PET scan, for the second time, showed "complete and total remission." Helain said, "God is good and greatly to be praised."

We, her fellow hikers, have experienced difficulties along our trails. One has had a hip replacement. Another's husband has Alzheimer's. One has kidney disease. But we always remember Helain's example. During her years of therapy, we never heard bitter complaints, self-pity, or angry doubts. It's true we prayed for her miraculous healing, but her extraordinary steadfastness taught us to endure and to believe. With our hiking poles planted firmly in our faith, we keep hiking. Beyond the next hill, we will find healing. "Wait, Helain, until we catch up."

<0><0><0>

Permission granted to the author by Helain Steele in 2016 to write Helain's story.

WOUNDED SOLDIERS

Wounded soldiers ripped apart

By the war, you didn't start.

Come to Healing Waters

All you sons and daughters.

Hurt by a horror we didn't see,

Join us for a chance to be

Blessed by Heaven above.

Anglers, filled with love,

Patiently teaching their art—

Fly fishing savvy they'll impart.

Pain soon turns to joy

When a soldier does employ

A cast too good to ignore,

And a fish begins to soar

Through air to the ready net.

The wounded soldier to get

And forget, for now, his sad regret—

Pain, terror his sorrowful debt.

<0><0><0>

Project Healing Waters Fly Fishing, Inc., is a special program designed to help with the healing of disabled veterans and active military service personnel through fly fishing outings and educational activities. In 2015, "more than 7,400 disabled veterans and disabled military service personnel participated in PHWFF program activities" (www.projecthealingwaters.org).

"Wounded Soldiers" was included in the 2016 publication *Sunrise Summits: A Poetry Anthology,* which features the works of the Northern Colorado Writers and was edited by Dean K Miller. *Sunrise Summits* was selected as a 2017 Colorado Book Award finalist.

READ ME A STORY

I ask her again, "Jennie, would you like me to read to you?" Frown lines appear on Jennie's pale forehead, which is framed by her white hair. I know that puzzled look. She wonders who this lady is? I look familiar, but she is proud and too often the right words, like names, have disappeared.

"Jennie, you remember, I'm your son Bob's wife. Recently we flew from our home in Lake Oswego, Oregon to Waukegan, Illinois to visit with you."

Jennie looks around as if she will see her son.

"Soon Bob will join us. He's meeting with the social worker. He wants to make certain that you are getting good care. Remember, yesterday you liked it when I read to you."

Jennie's large, strong hands continuously fold and refold the white washcloth on her lap. In the forty-some years, I'd known her, her hands were always busy working. They wrapped cards at the card factory. Those hands washed/set/combed out her friends' hairdos. They poured coffee for anyone who sat at her kitchen table. They created ceramic Christmas trees and crocheted angels for numerous gifts. The list was long. As a child, Jennie had barely finished sixth grade when she went to work in a factory to support her parents, five brothers, and a sister.

Several residents, seated nearby in what serves as the nursing home's large community room, say, "please read." With the barest of nods, Jennie agrees that I can read to her. Across the room, a large-screen TV flickers with Fred Astaire dancing and singing in the rain. A slight man bent forward, waves his cane and shouts, "I want my TV program, not this dumb movie." A tiny nurse enters and scolds him in Chinese-accented English. As she gently but firmly takes his elbow and leads him to his room, his incoherent reply fades away.

A woman says, "my place," at another woman seated on the gaily flowered loveseat. Unable to dislodge the intruder, she bangs her walker on the linoleum floor. A stocky aide with an accent, reminding me of grits smothered in molasses, lumbers over and calmly places her hands on the walker. "Now, Miss Janie, be good." Janie ignores her. "Honey, let's go to the dining room. You like the dining room." Miss Janie follows her.

Meanwhile, a lithe, middle-aged man passes by us pushing a cart filled with the patients' newly laundered clothes. In heavily accented Lithuanian, he greets us. I like Fred. Fred tells us how he once captained a Lithuanian ship, but now, he steers a clothing cart. He smiles at the irony.

I wonder what my mother-in-law thinks of her housemates and the international representatives that care for her. Is it more difficult for the caregivers to communicate in a new language or for the elderly, many suffering from dementia, impaired vision, or hearing loss, to get their needs satisfied? Hand gestures and touch seem to work in any language.

"Well, are you going to read or not?" Verna interrupts my musings. I adore Verna. She is Jennie's best friend.

"Sure, I think you'll like this story. It's about a nurse like you were."

"I can't be a nurse anymore because I'm blind. Jennie and I were schoolmates. Jennie and I are going to escape. We're going home. We're a team. She can see and drive, and I can give her directions."

"I know Jennie says she wants to go home. But the other day when we drove her to her old house on Fulton Avenue, she said it wasn't her home. I couldn't believe it. She acted as if she'd never seen the house she'd lived in for some fifty years. She wanted to go to her childhood home on Market Street."

I wonder what it would be like not to recognize your home of many years. It's as if Jennie's adult life disappeared. Now, all she has is her childhood.

"Jennie and I were schoolmates," repeats Verna. "We used to like to run up and down her mom's stairs. Didn't we, Jennie?"

My husband appears and bends down and kisses Jennie's cheek. "Hi, Ma. It's good to see you."

What does my husband feel when his mother doesn't know her son's name or that he is her eldest and only surviving child? Yesterday, she introduced him as her brother. At least, she knows they're related. How painful it must be for him.

"What did you have for lunch?" he asks. His mother stares at him, waiting for a clue. He continues, "Did you have soup, a sandwich?"

Bob is an engineer, a problem solver. He believes his small memory tests will help reactivate his mother's ability to recall.

Her mouth opens, "I had ah . . ." Her face flushed, frustration etched into every tense muscle, she taps her thumb and fingers together, as if pinching a word from the empty air.

To be helpful, he says, "The nurse said you had tomato soup. I'm glad to hear you're eating again. I worry that you're so thin."

She relaxes. I inhale and let go of some of the anxiety I feel. I wonder how frustrating it must be for her. She, who loved to talk, is losing whole chunks of the English language—gone—like her husband, five brothers, home, and almost everyone and everything else she loved.

I feel helpless. Like my husband, I wish I could do more to restore this remarkable woman I've grown to love and admire. It seems unfair.

With each visit, another part of her disappears. I remember my book. "Jennie, would you like me to read?" She nods, a serene look on her face. Her hands lie still in her lap. Close to God, I think, like his little children.

"This is a story from *Chicken Soup for the Soul*. You remember, the book I read to you last time."

How to End a Job Gracefully

How to end a job gracefully,

Better to end it forcefully.

To say leaving isn't fair,

You'd stay on a dare.

But then you acquiesce.

Can you do less?

For a lady knows when to go,

At the end of her show.

Your spirits may flag,

And your pain may drag.

You couldn't win,

And begin to spin.

To blast your way thru

And begin life anew.

TWENTY-NINE BALLOONS

Twenty-nine balloons, each bearing a name tag, rise slowly, like brightly colored polka dots against a blue felt sky. They represent a hard reality: 29 out of 109 of our classmates have died. I imagine what color my balloon might be at the next reunion. How fragile life is, like air escaping into the atmosphere. Empty-handed, we stand, frozen in small clusters, staring up as the balloons drift west above the Stratford Inn's roof. Although sated from our enormous brunch, the nearby bakery's sweet smells still tempt us, as if food could satisfy our queasy emotions.

"Look, they're all together," someone comments.

"Yeah, but there are a couple of stragglers trying to catch up," replies another. "Just like school."

Standing on the sidewalk, quietly we talk as if waiting for a funeral service to end. No one moves toward the waiting cars. For three days, we've met at the inn, celebrating the fifty years since our graduation, exchanging snatches of our separate lives.

At last night's event, as my husband and several men chatted, one said, "I never thought we'd be like the women talking about our health problems. Certainly not discussing our prostate problems."

I began to think of our class as an episode of television's popular *Survivor* series. One classmate had struggled with head and neck cancer. Another good friend had endured her son's painful divorce. She'd even forgiven her former daughter-in-law for a nearly fatal auto accident that injured her beautiful granddaughter.

Then, there was our class rebel. A man who had survived terrible war injuries and heart problems to astonish us with his many academic successes. His remarkable achievements were just one of the frequent success stories that lightened our hearts.

Three days of celebrating together had strengthened bonds once loosely defined by casual adolescence. At the same time, we reflected on classmate Reverend McConaghie's Saturday night blessing. He cautioned us about life's brevity and the need to commit ourselves to Christ.

The class of '58 keeps marching on: maybe not the most memorable of classes, but certainly, we've learned how to transcend life's challenges. Planted deep within us, like Sycamore's Midwestern agricultural roots, are strong values of independence, hard work, generosity, etiquette, loyalty, and community.

Even though some of us reside in distant states, we will return to celebrate the next class reunion. In the meantime, we hope there will be no additional balloons. We pray each member of the Class of 1958 will be blessed with good health and sufficient support to continue to thrive. We will meet again.

<0><0><0>

After the author's fiftieth high school class reunion, she wrote this story. In 2013, five years later, she returned to Illinois and lunched with many of her former classmates. In the meantime, the author's best friend, Joann, had died from an aggressive brain cancer. Although she grieved for Joann, she appreciated renewing a friendly companionship with those who came. Like adolescence, senior status was just another part of life's journey to be endured and hopefully, embraced.

BASED ON MAYA'S LIFE

Mommy, why don't you want me?

Please, I promise to be good.

I'm only three, can't you see?

Don't send me far away.

Not on a train with my brother,

Who is only five, all alone,

Far from our abusive mother,

We travel north to south.

Our kind, holy grandmother

Guides and teaches us.

Then, I return with my brother,

When I'm but thirteen.

Raped by mother's friend,

My voice tells my brother.

Others kick to death the fiend,

And now I fear my voice's power.

No more will I use speech!

I'll write notes instead, until

I'm told, "nations I'll teach,"

And so again I speak.

One night I arrive home late.

Mother hits me in my face.

Brother cries, "abuse isn't my fate,"

Mother begs forgiveness.

My friend is handsome, kind.

All night he beats me.

How could I be so blind?

Mother helps me heal.

It seems my back would soon break

From all the injuries, I've endured.

Forgiveness I choose, for my sake,

And give a gift from the offender.

<0><0><0>

This poem is loosely based on a replayed radio interview by Diane Rehm, on the *Diane Rehm Show*, of Maya Angelou, the famous poet, author, actress, and activist. Maya told how her mother sent her young brother and her, all alone, on trains from California to Arkansas and their deeply religious grandmother. When Maya and her brother returned to their mother's care, her mother's friend raped her. Later, her mother abused her. Then, Maya's boyfriend brutally beat her. When asked how she survived the abuse, she said, "I give a gift to someone from the offender. I'd get a bag of potatoes or other things, then give them away. I'd say they were from Joe or whoever I needed to forgive."

The author dedicates this poem to all of those who have suffered abuse.

SHOWDOWN IN ROOM 315

I'd barely begun my first teaching assignment when Dimitri, oversized for a tenth-grader, swaggered into my classroom ten minutes after the bell rang.

"You're late again," I said as I glanced up into his mischievous eyes scanning the classroom.

"I am? Go figure." Dimitri grinned at the class while a few snickered.

"This is your third warning." I waved three fingers at him.

"Aw teach, you don't mean it."

"The class is completing their grammar exercises. Take your seat. I don't want to hear any more from you."

While the students worked, I recalled my former professor's lecture on class discipline. If the teacher made the learning experience fun, he said, there would be no need for correction. I thought, fun, he should try teaching this class of thirty unruly teenagers. I felt like an imposter—a few months earlier I'd been the student. Although I felt insecure about my role as a teacher, I was excited. From the time I was a child, I'd played teacher with my younger sisters as the students.

A recent college graduate and newly married, I'd been both thrilled to teach and dismayed when assigned 150 sophomores and juniors, five classes each of thirty students. Committed to doing my best, in the few weeks since I'd started, I'd worked hard to improve their reading and writing skills—important attributes if they were to succeed in college or the workforce. Most students cooperated, but not Dimitri and his cohorts. How sad, I thought, Dimitri's annoying antics revealed to me a creative mind wasting away in a futile rebellion.

Laughter echoed from the back of the room.

"Dimitri Pollock, are you making that noise?"

"Not me, teach. I was just telling the others what a pronoun is."

The students tittered.

"Dimitri, you're disrupting the class. If you don't behave, you'll have to go to the vice principal's office."

Silence. Hot, humid air drifted lazily through the old school's unscreened, open windows—summer's final assault.

"I don't have to listen to you. And I'm not afraid of old Nolan either," Dimitri challenged.

A few boys laughed nervously.

"That's it, Dimitri. Go to the office. Now."

Agitated, he glanced at his friends, who looked away.

Once again, he gave me his silly smile, his apology.

How many times had I fallen for his charm? What if he and the other students didn't like me? On the other hand, if I gave in again, what would be the cost to the class and him? Anarchy, I thought.

"Go," I repeated, and pushed my chair back, stood up, and took several steps toward him.

"All right already. I'm going," Dimitri mumbled as he shuffled to the door.

After he had left, the class worked quietly. When the last bell rang, I gathered my papers and closed the door. I'd hoped to be a good teacher, maybe even inspire my students with my love of literature.

Feeling I'd failed Dimitri, I entered Vice Principal Nolan's office. An ex-marine, he said, "I ran into your Mr. Pollock on the stairs. When I asked why he wasn't in class, he started mouthing off saying he didn't *have to do anything*. I said, 'Okay, wise guy, you just earned yourself a three-day suspension. Get your stuff. And don't return until next Thursday.'"

As I drove home, I thought about Dimitri. I didn't hate him, but I had started thinking of him as Dimitri the Disrupter. For weeks, he and I had played a tug-of-war to determine who was in charge. While we struggled, the class was losing. Learning couldn't take place in chaos.

As I boiled water for our usual Friday night's spaghetti, I told my husband Bob about the day's events. Patiently, my poor husband had listened night after night as I recounted another of Dimitri's escapades. As I finished, our phone rang.

When I answered it, a woman's voice shrieked, "How dare you suspend my son!"

Startled, I moved the receiver away from my ear.

"My Dimitri is a good boy. Why are you picking on him? You . . ."

"If only Dimitri would behave—" I said when she interrupted me.

My husband mouthed, "Dimitri's mother?" I nodded. He grabbed the phone out of my hand.

"Mrs. Pollock, if your son gives my wife any more trouble, I'll beat the you-know-what out of him." He slammed the phone down.

"Bob, I can't believe you said that. Dimitri isn't a bad kid. The school custodian told me since his mom was divorced, Dimitri became the neighborhood bully. He probably wears her down as he does me. He needs a male role model. One he respects."

As we ate, I worried. What if the principal fired me? Not only did I love teaching, but we needed my income while my husband completed his studies.

Saturday morning, a subdued Dimitri surprised us by knocking on our apartment door. After we invited him in and sat at our kitchen table, he said, "My mother told me what you said, Mr. Strazer. She said I should apologize."

We chatted. Soon, Bob asked if Dimitri would like to go fishing with him. Eagerly, he agreed. When he returned to class, Dimitri quietly respected my authority. More fishing trips followed. Dimitri had the positive male mentor he desperately needed, and I had an orderly classroom.

When the new term began, I told my students what I expected from them. They needed to know my limits. Once they knew, I experienced only minor behavioral problems. We could even bend the rules and have fun on occasion. When things started to get unruly, a simple reminder and order soon returned. Mutual respect was far more important than whether they liked me. Defined limits enabled me to teach, and my students to learn.

As future students struggled to express their needs, each taught me something valuable. I'd always be grateful to Dimitri and my husband for teaching me my most important lesson.

POETRY SEEKS

Poetry hears

Heart's silence.

Poetry stretches

Person's pose.

Poetry searches

Soul's caverns.

Poetry eases

Life's hurts.

Poetry sees

Hope's design.

Poetry awaits

Love's touch.

Poetry knows

Faith's promise.

Poetry seeks

Truth's glimmer.

Poetry defines

Life's purpose.

<0><0><0>

"Poetry Seeks" was included in the 2016 publication *Sunrise Summits: A Poetry Anthology*, featuring the works of the Northern Colorado Writers, edited by Dean K Miller. Colorado Independent Publishers selected *Sunrise Summits* as a 2017 Colorado Book Awards finalist.

EIGHT THOUSAND MILES

Desert winds blew sand devils around us as we trudged behind a donkey cart loaded with our backpacks. We had arrived in Mali, West Africa, to visit our youngest child Mary, who was serving in the Peace Corps. Since Mali was a Muslim country, I'd followed Mary's advice and left my cross necklace at home, but now I felt vulnerable without it. What if my husband's fears came true? What if terrorists kidnapped us, held us for ransom like those tourists we'd heard about on the news? Or what if we were lost forever in the Sahel's barren landscape? There wasn't even a road to follow. We were putting our faith in Mary, who had only been in the country for two years.

Suddenly, a dark, slender man in army fatigues appeared. He shouldered his ancient rifle and discharged a mighty blast. Mary quickly explained, "He is just alerting everyone that you've arrived. You're the first volunteer's parents to visit."

Soon, surrounded by some four hundred singing and dancing villagers, they insisted that we lead what had become a parade into their village. When we arrived, the generous Malians gave us small handmade gifts. Tears rolled down my cheeks. I felt honored and appreciated—the opposite of what I'd felt nine months earlier when I'd felt pressured to resign from my job.

For twelve years, I'd worked at the hospital. One day they told me I was no longer needed. I understood that it was a cost-cutting move to replace me with someone with less experience and a lower salary. But my understanding didn't excise the wretched pain of feeling discarded and useless.

At sixty-two, what opportunities existed for someone my age? In the past, during similar budget cuts, I'd watched as other employees left, awash in bitterness. I refused to behave that way, no matter how scared I felt.

My mother often said, "Act like a lady." Despite my concerns, that is what I did. For a month, I cleaned my files and wrote detailed notes. I made it easy for a replacement to do my job. The program would continue, but I wouldn't. The most painful part of all was that no one would even notice my absence.

"Dear Lord, show me the way," I prayed. As He so often does, He answered through someone else, a fellow health educator at another hospital. When I shared worries about my future, she told me about a conference she had recently attended.

"I've just learned the most helpful tool," she said. "No matter what the situation is, there is an opposite, a benefit. Our typical response is to focus on the losses of job, marriage, home, or even health. Instead, the speaker told us to concentrate on finding what we gained with our loss."

At first, I resisted her advice as I grieved. I didn't care about "opposites." I wanted my job back. I missed my office, my co-workers, the routine. I missed the meaningful challenges of organizing health education classes for sick people. But as time passed, I grew tired of my dreary sorrow. Maybe I should try my friend's advice and seek some opposites.

The reverse of loneliness would be friendship. I called a neighbor and asked if she would like to take an exercise class with me. Soon, we became good friends. Although I missed my busy hours at work, I now had more personal time. I had choices. I tackled cleaning projects I'd delayed due to my long work hours. I volunteered at a mental health program.

Still, it wasn't until our trip to Africa that I understood the power of opposite thinking. We had cashed in our frequent flyer mileage and flown eight thousand miles to that village. We brought many presents—deflated soccer balls, Frisbees, pens, scarves, and inexpensive watches—believing we could improve the villagers' lives.

Instead, they taught us the opposite. Our lives were the ones that needed improving.

Despite living in mud huts without modern conveniences, running water, or sanitation, the villagers appeared content. Frequently laughing and greeting each other, the beautiful Malians truly cared for their neighbors. Although we slept on the ground in our daughter's tiny courtyard, I felt the peace I hadn't known since I left my job. I admired the Southern Hemisphere's brilliant stars and thanked God for bringing us here. I had expected we would spend our time helping the poor villagers.

Instead, they showed us that having less meant less to worry about and resulted in more time and energy for each other. These wonderful people of a different faith taught us an important lesson.

When we returned home, we decided we didn't need a large house. We sold it, gave away or stored most of our belongings, and left town in our twenty-two-foot trailer. It felt so freeing to have less to care for and so good to have more time for our family who needed us. We traveled to Illinois to attend to my mother-in-law, who suffered from dementia. After we had arrived, the nursing home staff decreased the numerous medications they'd administered to control her behavior. Family and friends once again enjoyed visiting her.

After she had died, we traveled. For a year we lived happily in our tiny trailer, while we looked for a new home with fewer expenses and lower state taxes. Eventually, we found a small mountain cabin in Colorado, near our grandchildren.

After my job loss, I thought they stole my life work from me. In seeking opposites, I discovered new opportunities that enriched my life. As I age, I still mourn when a new loss occurs, but soon, I seek its opposite. Always, I am rewarded.

<0><0><0>

"Eight Thousand Miles" was published in 2014 in *Chicken Soup for the Soul: Reboot Your Life.* In her introduction to *Reboot Your Life,* Claire Cook said, "You'll learn how to change your negative thoughts to their opposite along with Carol Strazer."

In 2016, Colorado contributors to *CSS* were invited to luncheons in different parts of the state, hosted by *Chicken Soup for the Soul* owners and editors. The editors told the contributors they were the lucky few to have their stories selected since *Chicken Soup for the Soul* receives about 5,000 submissions per publication.

Flying Lessons

One sunny afternoon I lay on a grassy knoll

And I looked up at the blueness above.

An osprey flew in graceful arcs.

His mate, too, drew an elliptical circle.

Ever higher they spun,

An aerial display for two.

Then, a smaller pair joined them.

Not as high, or with such finesse.

Still, parents flew and flew,

Winging encouragement.

How easy they made it seem,

Raising young in life's progression.

Would that we could do the same.

Author's Notes

These are my stories, and one "as told to me" story. I've written them as I remember them to the best of my ability. I've done my best to recreate events accurately as they occurred. I understand that everyone does not see the world through my eyes. The names of some people in my collection have been changed for their privacy. I stand behind the truth of the events and memories and hope for forgiveness if I have made mistakes.

Acknowledgments

I would like to acknowledge Teresa Funke, whose coaching and guidance were invaluable. I thank Jennifer Top for her editorial assistance. I appreciate the support of the Red Feather Lakes Writers, the Northern Colorado Writers, and the Sun City West Writers. I want to thank Mary Korte for her help in publishing this book. To anyone, I may have failed to include, please accept my deep apologies and my sincere thanks for your assistance in making this book a reality.

www.ingramcontent.com/pod-product-compliance
Lightning Source LLC
LaVergne TN
LVHW091223080426
835509LV00009B/1135